My Existence
Craves Yours

My Existence Craves Yours

Amna Dhanani

www.amnadhanani.com
Instagram: **amnadhanani_**
Facebook page: **amnadhananii/**
Twitter: **AmnaDhanani_**

ISBN 978-1-949773-00-2
Ebook ISBN 978-1-949773-01-9

Cover Vision by **Amna Dhanani**
Brought to life by **Mattias Fridh**
Editing by **S. H. Kazmi**

Acknowledgements

Thank you to my mom, for being my
inspiration and for her endless support
And for giving birth to me
Every time I thought the world had killed me.

To all of my family
(both by blood and by love)
For believing in me since the time
I didn't even know how to hold a pen.

To my friends for holding me up
Whenever I felt like giving up
And for literally holding me tight
Until I felt alright again.

To Aunty, Maano, Nomi Mamu, GB, Pomo
And S. H. Kazmi for sticking by my side
From the very beginning until the very end.

Special thanks to all Apas and Asif Bhai
For helping me reach this finish line.

Without you all,
This wouldn't have been possible.

Contents

I soak my words with blood
I thought I should let you know
Before you touch them
With your lips and read out loud.

Bittersweet Love

Amna Dhanani

The Call

Sometimes I feel as if someone out there
Is calling out to me
In words I don't understand
And a voice I don't know
Yet all too familiar to me.
Maybe my soul longs for him as well
That's why it pulls me towards him
This sound so blissful
But I don't know
Which direction it's coming from
So I'm sitting here and praying
For him to find me instead.

The Search

I've found many eyes seeking love
And I've seen many more seeking
understanding
But whenever I look into the mirror
Or go through any of my pictures
I find my eyes tirelessly searching for
something
As if it's my soul that is peeping through them
For an intangible haven
I'm not even sure exists.
A mysterious but familiar place
In someone to call home
Where it can finally rest and know that
My eyes won't have to search anymore.

Amna Dhanani

Smile

He looks at my smile
Like it brightens up his day.
I'm not oblivious to the fact that he likes me
But the question is
Why do I smile like this when I see him?

The Phase

My smile has fallen in love with me
Or maybe it's me who has?
I'm looking up at the ceiling
While my face hurts from all the exercise.
It's him in my mind
And in my heart as well I guess
But it's too early to say anything
Maybe it's just a passing phase.

Amna Dhanani

First Sight

I don't believe in love at first sight
But I think something clicked in me
When I first saw you.
You make me feel like I'm walking on clouds
But at the same time
You remind me that I'm afraid of heights.

The Untold Secret

I like you but I can't tell you
So I went to the ocean
To wash away my feelings
But the waves left them on the shore.
Perhaps the ocean was tired
Of all the secrets within.

Amna Dhanani

The Reason

I could be all drained of love
Pouring it out on your soul and drenching it
But still it wouldn't be enough
And nothing could be
Since you can't force someone
To feel what they don't
Just like you can't force yourself
To stop feeling what you do.

Undeniable Truth

How my heart fools my mind
That if I stayed strong a little longer
You could be mine
But the truth is undeniable
Even if I took the world
And brought it to your feet
Even if you felt the same as me
You wouldn't give in.

Scarred

You know I like you more than I should.
It has left me scarred
Deeper than you could ever see.

– I never learned to keep the truth in

Care

I know you don't need me
But let me take care of you anyway.

Amna Dhanani

Let Me Burn

If you won't let me put out the flames
Then let me burn with you.

Delusional

If it's an illusion
You and me
Then I'm happy to be called delusional.

Amna Dhanani

My Truth

You're my truth
And I follow you blindly.

Embrace

I want you to take me into your arms
Like the clouds embrace the moon.
Although I know
Just like them
You're only passing
Through my life.

The Sun

I fell in love with the sun
I thought I'd burn with love
Instead I burned for love.

The Sacrifice

Love never rained on my garden
So I sacrificed my tears for it
But you see
No rose blooms out of misery.

Amna Dhanani

Crime Scene

It flows underneath my skin
The love you said you didn't have for me
Then why do I feel
This connection between us?
Whenever we're in the same room
And you always seem to flee
Like it was a crime scene.

Avalanche of Love

Your love came
To me like an avalanche
And caught me
Completely off guard like one too.
I sank deeper and deeper
Under the bed of snow
The darkness engulfed my heart.
I was buried underneath
What people call beautiful.

Amna Dhanani

Certainty

I am certain about the uncertainty
That comes with you
But I don't know what to do with my heart
Which is absolutely certain that it wants you.

– I don't know how to give up on love

Trouble

I know I should've turned away when I felt it
I know I shouldn't have done what I did
I should have closed the door long ago
Instead of coming this far
'Cause the moment I saw you
I knew you were trouble
But that's the thing about me
I'm not afraid of troubles.

Amna Dhanani

Hesitated

Without any questions
Without any explanations
He gave in and I let him in.
He is finally in my arms
I feel happy but not relieved.

Desire

I killed you with my looks
And you killed me with your sigh
Which you let out as your defeat
Against your desires
And your sigh made me
Give into mine.

– Two murders in one day

Amna Dhanani

Worried

I'm not worried whether you'll hurt me or not
Because I know that you will.
I'm just worried about
How will you hurt me this time.

Tears

I wouldn't let a tear
Which fell for you fall down
So I took it from the corner of my eye
And left it on my heart.

Amna Dhanani

Silent Conversation

After our fight
I sighed and he smiled.
We communicated in silence
And understood each word.

The Storm

Often there's silence before a big storm
But this one looks like
It can make
The sweetest thing ever taste bitter.

– Love

His Words

I built my home on your words
Your actions demolished it right away.

– The few words he ever uttered

Liar

I lied for you
And you lied to me.

Amna Dhanani

Beautiful Lies

After nature
Your lies were the most beautiful.
I believed them like everyone believes it's day
When the sun comes out.

The Truce

I let him hold me from behind
Like it was a truce
But the truth is
I couldn't bear looking at him
After having heard the words
He had yelled at me that day.

Amna Dhanani

Empty of Love

I found the needle in the haystack
But I couldn't find love in your heart.

Drunk

I got drunk on your sorrow
While trying to keep you conscious.

Amna Dhanani

Unfaithful

I thought I was trying to keep 'us' afloat
But you weren't unhappy
You were unfaithful.

The Monster

He couldn't look into my eyes
After betraying me
Because he knew he'd see the monster
That the mirrors were unable to reveal.

Amna Dhanani

I Left Myself

I left myself to be with you
I don't think there's anything worse than that.

The Wall

With the wall between us
We were still too far and too close.
I wonder which reason made you leave.

Amna Dhanani

Afraid

Every second that I had you
I felt happy
But half of that every second
I was afraid of something going wrong.

Deaf

My love
For you
Was deafening
I couldn't hear the truth about you.

– I wasn't only blind

Amna Dhanani

Belief

I held on for far too long
Because I believed in a man you could be
And forgot about the man you were.

Your Memory

I proved you wrong
I stayed with your memory
Longer than you thought.

– Should I laugh or cry?

Amna Dhanani

Selfish

You were a bird
I had no wings.
Then you flew away
When your wounds healed.

Hollow

It's the tears that speak to me
In the middle of the night
The tears that come after a painful fight
The struggle of trying to get out of struggles
Have you never run in the dark, deep jungles?
Trying to run away
Trying to hide
With the shooting pain
Of no one being by your side.
Not everyone is as happy
As the perfect red wine
The stars seem sad tonight
Thus they shine
One shoots after another
Creating a beautiful view
While no one is aware
Of the torment they go through.
Have you never known the ache of the heart?
As your own love strangles you
Tears you apart
Loving someone so much
That it leaves you breathless
All your senses suddenly become senseless.
And then you realize
You are one of those fools
Chasing after a wild dream
Breaking all the rules

Amna Dhanani

But is it really your fault?
When all you did was love
Now I understand the rhyming pain
The poets speak of
The pain that comes in waves
In the oceans of sorrow
The fear of losing what I don't even have
Makes my heart hollow.

The Beast

His love woke the beast in her
She was fierce and she was wild.
Her love was a raging fire
He had never seen before
It flowed inside her like an endless ocean
But he didn't know how to swim.
It was an abyss
And he was afraid of the dark.
Her love knew no boundaries
Knew no limits at all
And it scared him
Scared him to his very core
But she wasn't something
That could be tamed.
In the end she gave him her all
And he gave her nothing
From that day on
That fire burned inside her
Like an eternal flame
A fire that burned even herself
Whenever she tried to put it out.

Amna Dhanani

The Halfway

I always said it's okay
Before you could utter a sorry
And I always texted you first
Without hesitation.
I knew what you needed
And when you needed it
I knew the timings like the back of my hand.
I took care of every little thing for you
Yet you used to complain about things
I had said.
You used to tell me what the problem was
It wasn't that I was yours completely
But it was that I was too much *there.*
The problem was that I was never angry
And that I was too often sad.
After blaming myself for so long I realized
My mistake wasn't loving you
Or loving too much
But whenever you walked towards me
I always met you on the halfway.

Moving On

I barely survived loving you
I don't know
How trying to forget you would be like.

Amna Dhanani

Blame

How could anyone blame me?
I hadn't known love
I only knew you.

His Name

I take his name
But it's not his name for me anymore
It means love to me
It's a synonym of love.
So when I wake up in the middle of the night
And I scream his name
I'm not calling out for him
I'm calling out for love
A love that I deserve
A love that is not him
His name
Has nothing to do with him anymore.
I've stayed with that name
For far too long to take it as it is
It always meant something more to me
Something that he never was
And now he is someone
I don't even recognize anymore
But somehow I recognize
The love I never got.

True Moments

I refuse to believe that everything was a lie
For some people change
And some show their real face.
I know that because
I've lived moments
That can't be staged.

Cup of Tea

It's okay if you failed to love me
I'm not everyone's cup of tea.

Closure

I happened to walk on the same path today
Where I used to carry you in my heart.
Everything was the same
Except you weren't there anymore.

– Not even a bit, not at all

Reclaimed

After being his for a long time
She finally reclaimed herself.

Growth

There's no point trying to find the girl
I used to be before I met you
Because even if I did find her
Which is rather impossible
She would fall for someone like you again.
I've changed for a reason
And I'm glad to have become
The woman I am now.

Surprised

We became friends immediately
As there was never a question about it.
Two completely different rivers
With the same perfect flow
But as our interests divided
And our habits matched
After years I find myself wondering
Could our hearts beat
In the same rhythm as well?
I was completely horrified by both my thought
And the smile which had just appeared
On my heart this time not just on my face.

Amna Dhanani

Cancer

My very being shook at the thought
Of my heart being in love again
While I still suffer from a cancer
That won't leave without taking me
Because once *he* lit a fire inside me
And I'm still surrounded by the fumes.

Freedom or Imprisonment?

Love is the only bird that can't be caged.
They say
"Blessed are those who are visited by her."
But often she leaves broken hearts behind.
Last time I met her on my balcony
And I was caged within my own heart
But this time she came and sat on my hand.
I wonder if this is a lucky sign
Or another imprisonment for my soul.

Amna Dhanani

Heartbreaks

After so many heartbreaks
They assumed she doesn't know
How to love anymore
But in truth
It came to her before breathing.

Loving for her
Was always easy.
The only reason she stayed away
Was because she didn't know
How to stop once she started
To love someone.

Lost and Found

Lost in the thoughts of you
I walked towards the place where we first met.
I didn't even realize I was walking
Until I found more memories of us
Waiting for me there.

Amna Dhanani

Photograph

I never understood
Why anyone would kiss a photograph
Until I was so desperate to feel you
And did the same.

*– You're that smile that doesn't wear off from my
face*

His Existence

He was standing there
And it took me by surprise
That was all I ever needed.

– He only had to exist to make me happy

Amna Dhanani

In Love Again

I just wanted the loneliness to be gone
And he filled my existence in a way
That I have fallen in love again.

Perfectionist

I love you
I love you for the very reason
That you're not mine
Because whatever I touch
I break it.
Whatever I lay my eyes on
It turns into a mess.
Whatever I try to fix
It turns into a disaster.
So I see you and love you with my heart
Because you're perfect.
I love you because ironically
I'm a perfectionist.

Amna Dhanani

Dream

I know I can't have you
So every dream of you
Is a dream that came true.

– Me and you, too good to be true

Longing

I wonder if dreams are only there
To give us a taste of what we cannot have.

Amna Dhanani

My Heart

I took my heart out in front of him
I let him see the pieces of my heart
Piercing into the parts that were still whole.

Strength

Her eyes were held up into his
Even as tears rolled down
He had never seen such strength before.

He was mesmerized
And I thought to myself
To save me from this life
He has to become my life.

Amna Dhanani

Language of Our Souls

The eyes speak the language of our souls
I'm not fluent in it but I think
Yours wants to connect with mine.

The Beauty

The beauty of our love story is
No one knows
Not even us.

Amna Dhanani

Burden

I love you
You don't have to say anything.
It's my burden to bear
And I'll bear it
You only had to know the truth.

Shared

He finally let his body loose
As if a huge weight
Had been lifted off his shoulders.
I never noticed before
What he carried with him
From the day when we first met.

"I think it was your laughter
If not then definitely your voice.
How can I explain this to you?
I'm not the writer, you are.
I was never good at expressing what I felt
But I know this much
Staying up with you
When I needed to wake up early
Learning your favorite songs
So I could make you happy.
In which way can I tell you?
It's not a burden that you carry
And even if it is
We both share it now."

Amna Dhanani

The Inevitable

It was inevitable for us to fall for each other
As it is inevitable to fall apart one day.

Withered Tree

Oh withered tree
I want to give you my love
Not in hope to give you back
The greenery you've lost
But only to truly accept
The form disliked by others
Just because you don't sustain their needs
I love you for the life you still hold.

Amna Dhanani

Broken Heart

A broken heart is so beautiful
I wonder how anyone can resist
Falling in love with it.

One of a Kind

I wonder how people see
The one they love in other faces.
There's no one that looks like you or could
You are one of a kind for my eyes and my
heart.

Amna Dhanani

You and I

You and I
Are day and night.
We meet when everyone's either asleep
Or too busy to notice
At sunset and sunrise.

Someday

I think I was only shattered
So that at least my pieces could find a home
As I couldn't when I was whole.
One day he found them scattered
And gathered all of them.
Now he keeps them in his heart
Safely guarded in his chest.
Maybe, just maybe
If I were put whole again someday
I'd call him my home.

Amna Dhanani

Revival

You revived me
When I didn't even know I was dead.

Every Day

Even though we haven't touched
I've felt every part, every inch of you
I've felt your presence in every day.

At dawn
When the cold wind embraces my body
It leaves me defenseless just like you do.
I see you and then
I see the world in a different way
I live crazy every day
And yet somehow you make me crazier
I'm open to everything
I've never done before.
Every day I skydive in love with you
And I fall deeper and deeper every day.

In the morning
When you're getting late for work
You fix your hair quickly with your fingers
Without intention
You scratch your light beard.
I've watched you a lot of times to know
How touching you would be like
I've daydreamed about this every day.

In the evening
When twilight dances goodbye

Amna Dhanani

At the middle where the sun
Melts into the ocean
And the moonlight starts to uncover its face
The moon swears to be
The witness of our love.
From the sun's journey to the moon
Your essence I feel every minute of every day.

At night
The bed may seem empty
But I lie there
With your fragrance in my blanket.
It's your touch
That makes me and my heart warm
Then how can we say we have never touched?
When our hearts have
And our souls are connected
It's something that
Physical touch can never compare to.

Home

He started to come close
My heart started to race.
He whispered into my ears "May I?"
And so many images rushed into my mind
As I nodded my head
He looked into my eyes
Then he slowly put his head on my bosom
And fell asleep holding my waist.

– We were both home for the first time

Amna Dhanani

Oblivious

Let me take your breath away
Trust me
You won't even notice it's gone.

The Kiss

My lips met a pair of their kind
Warm, fierce and desperate
For the love that kissed us goodbye.

Was it a moan in pleasure?
Or a groan from your bite?
Or in relief I let out a sigh?

I wonder if we created a memory
To remember and cherish
Or to regret and cry.

All I know is I've made love to you
I've touched your body as if my own
And kissed you until my lips were dry.

Whisper

I whisper your name ever so softly
This is my way of kissing your soul.

Reassurance

When he kisses my forehead
I feel like he's reassuring my soul
There is someone who really cares.

Amna Dhanani

Sweet Gestures

You sing to me with your heart
And I write about you with love.

Purest Form of Love

You sleep in my arms like a baby
While your arms hold me tight like a man.
You make me feel both safe and needed.

*– I found the purest form of love in your sleepy
smile*

Amna Dhanani

By My Side

Last night I dreamed about you
And I woke up to find you by my side.
I don't remember being this happy before.

My Fairy Tale

You will still be my fairy tale come true
Even if we don't have a happily ever after.

The Agony

The Bittersweet Evening

Today I went out
For the first time in weeks since we parted.
When I felt the evening sun on my face
And I closed my eyes
It was almost as if you touched my face
The warmth was almost as soothing
As your hand.

The beautiful birds were bathing in the pond
But I was lost in my own thoughts, so lost.
Our memories were coming back to me
One by one
As I stared at the sun's reflection in the water.
The flashbacks
Were playing at my heartstrings
The raw pain was tearing me apart
Into tiny pieces
And I stood there
Stunned by the beauty and the pain
Frozen in fear of what already had happened.
Isn't it funny?
The terror in your stomach doesn't leave you
Even after it's over
It feels like you were kicked in the guts.

On top of that
The memories were all sweet

Amna Dhanani

You treated me right
You held me so tight.
Every morning you found something
To compliment me on
No matter how messed up I looked
All you saw was me
The way you looked at me
As if I only belonged in your eyes.
Your bewitching smile used to be
The best part of my *every day.*

We lived in the moment as best as we could
Knowing it would end
We embraced the opportunity
We bravely lived through and beyond the fear.
Everything was more than perfect
Except one thing
It had to end and so it did
Leaving us as two halves of a broken heart.

They talk about how you meet someone right
When the timings are just so damn wrong
But with us
The timing may never be right
No matter how perfect we were for each other.
Now all is left for us are our memories
Whether I look at the stars or the moon
It reminds me of you.

My Existence Craves Yours

And the moon
The moon was the sole witness of our love
Although the evening sun
Made me feel even closer to you.
Not only that
But that's how much time we had
The time between the evening and the sunset
What beautiful and magical moments
We were given
And it was the best time
Of both our lives so far.

Amna Dhanani

Homeless

For months your breathing was my lullaby
And your voice was my cradle.
I've not only been sleepless
But homeless without you.

Escaped

More than anything I want love
And it escapes me every time.

Amna Dhanani

4 Am Voice

I don't know how to fall out of love
With your 4 am voice.

Destruction

I thought I was in love with you
But I was wrong.
I always fall in love
With my own destruction
And that's what has happened again.

Denial

I have never been in love before
If I had been
It would have never hurt like hell.

Your Memories

Your memories make me choke
In the middle of the night
When I try to hold back the tears
While my heart drowns in them.

Unsheltered

It was your love I spoke so fluently
Now when others try
To comfort me with their love
I don't understand a word.

– I feel like a roof without its walls

Sweetest Home

I lived into your thoughts
And that was the sweetest home I ever had.

Amna Dhanani

Proof

I blinked and you were standing
On the other side of the river again
But the ashes of the bridge were proof enough
That it wasn't a dream at all.

A Snowflake

Even though I know
A lifetime with you wouldn't be enough
But our moments were cut too short
As if a snowflake fell on my hand
And melted as soon as it touched
Yet I lived in those moments
As if those were the only ones I lived.

Amna Dhanani

Dust

I never learned to go halfway and return
I'm either all in or nothing at all.
That's how I got my heart broken
But still I gave you each and every piece
And you returned them back to me as dust.

– But I know you didn't mean to

Resemblance

You know there's something similar
Between you and the rain.
You both pull me back together
Before breaking me again.

Amna Dhanani

Blank Eyes

How can it be?
There's a starlit sky
And yet my eyes stare at my lap.

– What have you done to me?

Drowning

I already lost you once
Losing your memories wasn't an option
So I live and die every day
By drowning in them.

Amna Dhanani

Snow Globe

I watched you stepping backwards
Through the door
Someone pressed the rewind button
On the dance floor.
All of a sudden it felt like
We never had this dance
Against life
We never even stood a chance.

We came this close
For having it all and then some
Our bodies became one as we waltzed
On the song we used to hum.
What a beautiful sky
And ground covered with snow
Inside the snow globe
We danced slow.

You and I
A perfect groom and bride
Nothing else mattered
Since you were by my side.

What a perfect night
How sad that's all it was
The clock ticked and tocked
So we had to pause.

My Existence Craves Yours

Since the sun is rising
We'll go back to being dolls
And now on the snow globe
The curtain falls.

But don't despair
As another night will come
The play button will be pressed
And once again we will become one.

– To be continued...

It will continue in You were the Soul to my
Existence book

Amna Dhanani

Our Loss

I'm not going to beat up myself anymore
For the choices you made
But I can't deny the fact that
It wasn't only your loss.

Forgiveness

I forgive you because
You had no choice.
I forgive you because
This isn't what you wanted either.
I forgive you because
Parting ways is just as painful for you
As it is for me.
I forgive you because
That's the last thing I could do for you
Although I'm not sure
If forgiveness is a blessing for you
Or a nightmare
That'll haunt you for as long as it wishes to.

Amna Dhanani

Fade

We filled every mundane thing
We ever did with love
Making it special.
As everything slowly started
To fade between us
I never thought that
Your love too, would fade
But one day it did.

– Please tell me it didn't

Failure

There was no moon tonight
Nor was he by my side
So I went to the beach
And watched the anxious waves
Thrashing here and there.
They were not in harmony
Like they used to be
So I sang a lullaby for them
Trying to calm both the ocean
And my heart
But I guess I was no moonlight
Or a song in his voice
So I failed us both.

Amna Dhanani

Caught Off Guard

Your name crashes at my heart
Like the waves crash on the shore
Except that the shore is always ready
And my heart is always caught off guard.

Eclipse

Their love story was called an eclipse
What could be more tragic?

Illusions

They don't realize what they've lost
It's just one of those illusions from fairy tales.

Happiness

Happiness knocks at my door
And runs away before I can open
Just like those naughty kids in the
neighborhood.

Amna Dhanani

Tragic End

Fairy tales are real
I've seen them happen for others
But when it comes to me
It's a tragic end to a mystery.

Hurting

Just because you're strong
Doesn't mean you're not hurting.

Amna Dhanani

Expectations

People expect so much from my heart
It's still beating, isn't that enough?

Suffocation

I want to breathe in the air
Which doesn't suffocate me
Each time I inhale.

Amna Dhanani

Disappear

And this time
She closed her eyes
Not to wish for sleep
But to disappear
In the same darkness
That won't let her sleep
To escape the light
The light that won't let her
Disappear.

The Darkness

There's a different kind of darkness
Which surrounds my life
For me the sun doesn't decide
When it's the day.

Amna Dhanani

Living with Depression

There are a lot of people
Who don't get what depression is.

It can occur a lot of times during each day
A feeling, a need to drop dead
In the middle of nowhere
Just stop right there
And let yourself be
Pretend that you're not there.
Block every incoming voice like it's not real
Whether it's traffic
Your loved ones calling out to you
Or your crying baby.
The only thing that seems real
Is this one voice
Or are there many?
It differs from person to person
On what tortures them more.
So this voice invites you into the darkness
It pulls you in
Like it's the only thing you've ever wanted
A deep sleep but it's a fake promise
The whole time you're wide awake
In a pitch-dark room.
You see the light and you can reach it too
But the voice convinces you otherwise
It tells you this is where you belong

My Existence Craves Yours

And slowly it becomes so easy
To leave everything
And lie there like nothing matters
Just like you don't matter
Which is once again a lie.
It's so easy to become convinced
That you don't exist for anyone
Nobody cares about you.
And even if they prove they care
The voice will make you feel
You're not good enough for them.

Let me tell you
This is not the worst thing
That happens in depression
There are a lot of phases I've just started one.
Everything could be going well
But when it hits you
It feels like everything is over.

So please, I'm asking you
If someone tells you
They're suffering from depression
Do not take it lightly or joke about it
It's a serious problem
That can happen to anyone
And it's not their fault.

– How I've lived with depression

Amna Dhanani

Depression

Inside my home, I was out of place.
For the society, I was out of shape.
Other girls mocked me, I was out of fashion.
My teacher told me, I was out of line.
My friends complained, I was out of sight
My lover exclaimed, I was out of my mind.

I belonged nowhere with no one.
No one accepted me the way I was
No one knew why I did what I did
No one even tried to understand.

And then they say you're not alone
Because you've got a family
And a place called home.
They tell me to look at the less fortunate
But is it really going to solve
Any of my problems?

My depression has been taken lightly
And so has been my anxiety.
If I have suicidal thoughts
It's still my fault
Because I can't be happy with more blessings
Than my fingers and toes.

– How I've seen depression around me

The World

People who ask me why I am depressed
Aren't ready to hear the truth.
It's what we call 'normal' in this world
It can be something big and small both
It doesn't always have to be attached
To a big tragedy
And when I tell them that
Their reply often sounds like
"That's what most people have to deal with
That's how the world is."
That's the reason exactly
Because the world should not be like that.
Depression doesn't mean I can't deal with it
I have depression
Because I am dealing with it.

Amna Dhanani

Demons

They said I've conjured up my demons
I guess they forgot
To look into the mirror this morning.

Fighting Depression

I'm too busy fighting my depression
To actually fight it off.

Amna Dhanani

Anxiety

Anxiety takes away the privilege
To enjoy the present.
It's the worst kind of punishment
For those who prefer living in today
Instead of dwelling in the past
And worrying about the future.

Anxiety Attack

Dried lips
Agonized eyes
Unsteady breathing
Palpitating heart
Anxious body
Restless soul.

Amna Dhanani

Eternal Hunger

How do I eat?
Even when I look at my favorite food
I'm repulsed by it
It's supposed to smell delicious
But I get nauseous.
Even if I forcibly put a morsel into my mouth
My throat blocks its entry to my system
As if it's swollen
Because of all the anxiety in my every cell.

– My mom complains I don't eat enough

Dreaded Nights

At night
My mind makes me feel like
I'm not on my own bed.
All of a sudden
My pillow becomes a rock
I can't relax
I can't get comfortable
As if any minute I can be called off
As if any minute I will realize
There's a place where I had to be
And I'm running late.
Every inch of my body
Wants to be at some place
I don't have the address of
As if it's not my bed but a bus station
And I'm waiting for my ride to arrive
But this bus isn't a synonym for the morning
I'm not waiting for the morning
To start the vicious cycle of life
All over again
Which I had barely managed to escape from
Because night means it's too late
To be around people
To keep working
To keep struggling.
It's finally time to accept the darkness
As my only relief

Amna Dhanani

And yet my eyes wouldn't close
Instead I live a nightmare
With my eyes wide open.
They're heavy, they're tired
And I'm sleepy
Yet I'm not able to close them
As if there's a clock
On every wall of my room
Reminding me of the time
When I have to get up.
The past snores loudly
In the back of my head.
The worries of future blast music
Giving me a headache.
Anxiety has replaced peace in my present
So I lay awake on the bed of my thoughts
With a drained mind
A frightened heart
An aching body
And a tired soul.

25 Years

When someone asks me what's wrong?
What is bothering you?
How am I supposed to answer?
What am I supposed to say?
That the result of existing
Living and everything else
In between for 25 years
Has left consequences for me.
Everything I've endured
Has left an everlasting impact
On my being.
There's just too much for me to bear
And yet it's not something huge
As they might be expecting.
No, no one close to me died
I didn't get my heart broken
I didn't fail any exam
Or lost my dream job.
It was something as trivial as a tight sleeve
That won't come down after an ablution
Which gave me a panic attack.
I chose to bath today
My anxiety chose to stay with me
For 4 hours.
The heat has got me so low
I won't stop sweating
I can't keep working

Amna Dhanani

Like a normal person would.
My breath decided to suffocate me
For 2 hours straight
Because when electricity went off
It took a few moments
Before the generator could start.
The truth is
I have got nothing to tell you
Except that tragedies of my life
Have left me completely wounded
And I don't even know how or why.
All those things I've moved on from
Have given me depression
Which always stays with me now.
How am I supposed to give you an answer?
Which is worth your time.
I choose to answer
"I'm okay now." instead
Or that I will get okay
Because I can't and won't lie.
And yet despite all that
I am one of the strongest people
You will ever get to meet.
I can say that about myself because
I'm the only one who has witnessed
Every second of those 25 years of my life.

The Battle

There's a battle going on inside of me
With me
For me
And because of me.

Caged Bird

Limitless potential
Life grounded.
Talented hands
Tightened chains.
Compassionate soul
Apathetic world.
Love-filled heart
Deceiving creatures.
Upbeat personality
Tormenting surroundings.
Open minded
Caged bird.

Freedom

I've often seen others choosing waves
As an example for freedom
But I wonder why do they keep crashing
On the shore if they are really free?

Amna Dhanani

Trapped

My ropes aren't as loose as they seem
I'm allowed to fly but my legs are tied up.
I can only go as up as to see the world living
But never far enough to live in it.

Who Am I?

I'm not as innocent
As my eyes suggest
Or as bad
As the thoughts in my mind.
I'm not broken
Like my heart is right now
And I'm not so worn out
As my exhausted body
Nor I am as strong as my soul is.
So who am I
Between all these fragments of me?
If I'm not good or bad
Weak or strong
Who am I as a whole?
If I'm whole at all.

Amna Dhanani

Gone

The moon is the only one I can call mine
But like everyone else
It's only there for some time and gone in rest.

The Irony

Even if in the moment
We mean when we say 'always'
It can always change in the future.

Amna Dhanani

Taken for Granted

When I go out of my way for anyone
They almost immediately remind me
Why I shouldn't.

*– I don't know how to be myself without being
taken for granted*

Healer's Attack

When I look back
I often wonder to myself
How can it be?
That the people who once
Tried to heal your wounded heart
Later on become the reason
Behind your broken heart.

Amna Dhanani

Broken Bridge

She burned the broken bridge
Instead of fixing it
In hope that somebody might find her.
That's a mistake she'll never make again
She swore as she swam out of the river
In the cold night.

I Live

Amna Dhanani

Living

I've survived a lot more
Than I'd like to admit.
No one knows the whole story
Of anything I've gone through
Not even those who live with me.
But yes, I've survived
I'm surviving
And by the will of God
I will continue to survive.
But there's one question
Which has always bothered me
If I'm living or not?
And I can finally answer myself
Yes I am.

– *All praise is due to God*

Survivor

I refuse to be called a victim
Even if I were
I wouldn't go down without a fight.
That alone makes me a fighter
Not a victim
I'm a proud survivor.

– I fight to survive, I don't fight to win anymore

Amna Dhanani

Progress

I was broken into a million pieces
But every piece of me has survived.
One of these days
I'm going to be put whole.

– I'm a work in progress

Survival

I made the best out of everything
That came my way
That's how I have survived for so long.

Amna Dhanani

My Journey

I started my journey late
And I walk on my path slowly.
There's no telling
When I'll reach my destination
But I know one thing for sure
If I give up
It's guaranteed I'll never reach it.

Comfortable

Now I can be okay with myself
For not being okay.
It took me years to feel comfortable
In my own skin whenever I feel low.

Amna Dhanani

I Choose to Live

It hurts more because
I choose to live not just exist.

Fight for Freedom

Freedom has to be fought for.
Sometimes you even have to fight
With yourself for it.

Amna Dhanani

Reborn

I've died a million times
Before I was born with strength.

It's Time

Your sadness and sorrow
Can I borrow?
But I can't promise
I'll give them back.
I'd hide them somewhere
Even you can't find
The pain you've lived
Your whole life.
It's time to be happy
It's time to smile.
You're not useless or worthless
But a gem in disguise.
So chin up, my darling
Good days are coming.
Bath, get dressed
And pack your bags.
We leave tomorrow morning
To never come back.

Amna Dhanani

Look Within

When you're searching for happiness
Look within your life
Within yourself.
The outer world can often be
A good illusion of happiness.

Self-Love

I saw someone in the mirror
Smiling at me today
So I smiled back even wider.

Amna Dhanani

You're All You Need

You don't need anyone
Until you start telling yourself that you do.

Honest Conversations

I miss those conversations
Where there were no hidden meanings
In simple sentences
Every word meant exactly the way it was.

Amna Dhanani

Ego

If they don't call or text you
Don't think that
You haven't made an impact on their lives.
It's not about how long
You've been there with them
But how long they've had their egos for.

Stop

Learn to stop saying it's okay
When it isn't.

Amna Dhanani

The Courage

Don't blame yourself
For choosing to see the good in people.
Don't feel bad
Even if they chose to see the bad in you
Even if sometimes
They chose to see the things
That weren't even there.
It takes a lot of courage
To not give up on someone
Especially
When everything inside of you aches.
Don't regret anything
You did what you thought
Was best at the time.
You're not an idiot
To love someone that intensely
Someone who lets you go after that, is one.

– Everyone that I ever loved

Devotion

In today's world
Total devotion and selflessness
Towards something or someone
Is seen as foolishness
When it should be admired and cherished.

– Rare is the odd one out

Amna Dhanani

Willingness

You can only make someone understand
If they're willing to.

Priority

You are not selfish to put yourself first
However the way you do
Changes everything.

Amna Dhanani

Maturity

Maturity isn't about knowing
And understanding what others don't.
It's about acting upon that knowledge.

Imperfection

Imperfection is
What makes everything beautiful
Whether it is art or people
It makes us special.
We all come with our sets
Of strength and weaknesses
Just like a beautiful flower
Not all the petals are the same size or shape
And that's what makes it unique.

Amna Dhanani

We Are All Humans

I don't understand racism.
Every person goes white in the face
When they're in shock
And all of us go red in the face
When we blush.
We all are humans
There's no difference.

Live Freely

The world is a chaotic mess in itself.
Do not worry
About your mess being the spotlight
Live freely.

Amna Dhanani

Modern Art

I'm not a mess!
I'm modern art!

Memories

Live to make memories
Which make you laugh
Where you're *not* supposed to laugh.

Amna Dhanani

Dance

Let me dance with your doubts
And turn them around.

Positive Outlook

Don't underestimate a positive outlook
It can turn problems into solutions.

– Feel like giving up? Give up the negativity

Amna Dhanani

Walk with Confidence

Enter the room believing
That your smile will light up the place
And it will.
Own your imperfections
Like you chose them yourself.

Live Out Loud

Not only laugh out loud but live out loud
Hell, I even think out loud and get in trouble.

Optimism

I'm married to optimism
I sometimes cheat on it with negativity.

Feel

I'm not a know it all
I'm a feel it all.

Risk-Taker

I take risks even when I shouldn't
Because for me
Pain is better than a monotonous life.

*– I create my own ripples instead of going with the
flow*

Liberation

It doesn't matter
How many big goals I achieve
I've always found my heart
More rejoiced at the little things of life.

*– The small things in life can be so liberating for
your soul*

Amna Dhanani

I Want to Live

People don't believe
When I tell them I have depression
Because when I laugh
I laugh with my heart
And when I live
I live the smallest things to the fullest
Because if I have to live in the suffering
Then I want to live in the happiness too.

Every Drop Matters

It's not a glass half full
Or half empty scenario with me.
It's more like
As long as there's a drop left
The game is on.

Amna Dhanani

Moonlight

The moonlight represents my strength
No matter how many clouds come and go
She pierces through them
If not that night then definitely the next.

Phases of Life

Day and night don't only represent 24 hours
These are the phases of our lives.

Amna Dhanani

Peace

The peace that we search for
In all the quiet places
Is often found in the noise of nature.

Wind

Out of all the wonders of nature
I love wind the most
Because the moment when it touches you
That moment cannot be captured
With a camera but with your heart.

Amna Dhanani

Twilight

How ironically beautiful is that
The shadow of the sun is also light
Twilight.

Phases of the Moon

It's so easy to love the moon in its full form
But I love the moon
Even when it goes through its phases
From day one to the last day of the month
When it's still there but no one is aware
Of its existence or beauty.
And especially the night before the full moon
It shows the strength of coming so far
And that's really inspiring.

Amna Dhanani

The Date

The moon and I had a date last night
We made it casual
He was dressed in clouds
I was in my pajamas.
We talked for hours and hours
Just through eye contact
And the stars were shy of us.
Finally when I was tired
And closed my eyes
The moonlight kissed my forehead
And wished me goodnight.

The Stars

They twinkle
As if it's the last night for them
They twinkle
As if they were made just for us to look at.
The shine of the moon is however bright
But never could dim the brightness of this sky.
It feels like
As if the moon was only there
To compliment them
As if the beauty of the moon is incomplete
Without the sparks
As if the night itself will miss their shine
As if the sky would be lonely without them.
Their beauty I could never comprehend
Each and every one of them
Is unique in their own way.

Amna Dhanani

The New Beginning

The purple sky roared at me
Its rage could not be contained
The lightning danced with the wind
And the rain fell out of fear
But I've never felt freer
As if the thunder spoke
To the thunder inside of me.
When two storms got together
The world was in chaos
And my smile became a new beginning.

The Words

Questions

So many people ask me the reason
For becoming a writer
And a lot more ask questions
Based on my sad poetry
If I've lost someone I loved?
Or if I'm heartbroken?
A writer can channel emotions
Shape them with a different mold
And write however they would want to.
It doesn't matter if the pain is relevant
To the words they write.
The most important thing for writing is
To be able to feel love
And passion inside of you with an intensity
Through others, inspired by some place
Or a memory and for me
The source of inspiration is pain
And nature more than anything else.
It can be a lot of little things too
It can be based on something I've witnessed
Not only based on my own experience.
So here is the answer
To the question most asked about me
A tragedy doesn't always give birth to a writer
But it can inspire them
Whether it's their own or not.

Warrior

I'm a warrior and my weapon is a pen.

How strange it is
That I don't use my weapon
To attack or defend
But merely to survive.
I refuse to disappear
As a lifeless soul
That wanders about this Earth.
I'm a warrior
I'm a writer but most importantly
I'm a human being who deserves to live.

Amna Dhanani

Bleeding Words

It's not my fault that I bleed words
And together they take a form of a sea.

Mother

She is a mother
She nurtures her words
So that they make a difference in the world.

Amna Dhanani

Souls in Need

There are so many feelings
I want to share with the world
But I'm afraid
They won't reach the souls in need.

Blank Pages

The blank pages scream to me
The emptiness tortures them every second
And I know how that can be
So I try to fill every one of them.

Amna Dhanani

Consumed

I'm consumed by my own words
If they come out
They're heavier than the scales
If they remain inside
It's as disastrous as if the world
Is coming to an end.

Free Yourself

We all communicate through words
And yet writing is a skill
Not many people have.

*– Free yourself, write down the words that hold
you captive*

Amna Dhanani

Silence

Silence is
Unspoken yet loud.
Empty yet crowded.
Peace yet torment.
Contemplation yet blank.
Truth yet deceit.
Choice yet forced.
Numbness yet overwhelming.

Silence is one of the most meaningful words
Which holds a lot of power within.

Darling Pages

You are my canvas
You, my darling pages
I'm painting you with my words
With you, I can portray my feelings
Which are wilder than my handwriting.
I'm sure they give you more beauty
Than you had being perfectly blank
Because now that you're imperfect
Like the rest of us
Your beauty seems real
Just like my pain.

– Sometimes I write when I'm betrayed by my own feelings

Amna Dhanani

Pen and Pain

I see the world and its pain
That's how my pen takes my hand
And forces me to write
But when I see its beauty
I take the pen
Push aside the pain
And force myself to write.

My Roof

I built my home on the words I wrote
Even if they're broken
They're something of my own.
I'm not afraid anymore as it's a home
Where the roof can't be taken by others.

Amna Dhanani

Inspiration

The pain you gave me
Became my inspiration to write.
You see I can take negative
And turn it into positive
And you thought you could keep me down.

– To the past

The Terror

All the pages that I've ever written
Which were the most painful ones?

The ones I wrote
While my tears were falling on the words
And smudged them
Making them hard to understand.

Or the ones I personally had no emotions for
But still each letter screamed
For an escape from each other.

Or the goodbye letters
I never gave to certain people
Because we said goodbyes
Without saying goodbyes.

Or those unfinished poems I knew
Which were never going to be completed.

Or the ones where the ink was my own blood
Which had blackened
From my sobs, fears and heartbreaks.

I guess I will never find out
Because at the time of writing them down
These all were intensely felt

And the pain was unbearable.

Or maybe the blank pages
Are the most painful ones in my life?
Which ache to be filled
The emptiness
The uncertainty
Which springs the horror
Of endless possibilities.
And then there's the terror
Of always remaining unfilled
Which beats everything else.

Salt Water

I drag around the words
Which are heavy on my soul
I refuse to shape them into poetry
Where they truly belong with the rest
Because your mention doesn't deserve at all
To be written down with such care
As I caress the words
With the tip of my pen softly
To comfort the pain
They might've felt in my heart.
But I do deserve closure
One way or another
So I let you out through my eyes
The same eyes
Through which you entered my heart once.
I was as successful as the sea will ever be
At getting rid of the salt from its water.

– Some wounds I don't talk about

Amna Dhanani

Our Relationship

Our relationship is simple
I write, you read.
You cry, I feel.

Thank you

You've come all the way here
You've made my journey worth living.
You've made every word that I bled, precious
You've counted the tears I shed.
My writing is not only my passion
But my therapy and as a part of my therapy
There have been many times
When I wanted to scream to the world
What I felt but I couldn't
So I wrote it instead.
My words are the voice
That'll reach the people I couldn't
So I thank you for giving wings to my voice
And for letting my words breathe.
I thank you with all my heart
For your understanding
Just by listening to what I had to say
You've shown respect
And love to the most delicate parts of me.
I thank you for reaching
The end of one fragment of my soul.
I didn't think this day would ever come
But I hoped, oh how much I hoped
That one day my voice
You've never heard
Would tell you tales of how I've felt
And then these unheard feelings

Inside these words won't be hidden anymore.
And I had hoped that you, yes you
Could resonate with them
Even if it's just one poem
Even if it's just about pain
My pain, your pain, our pain
It makes us special
It makes us unique to have felt it
The way we did.
This is our story
Neatly wrapped within a poem
That has more tales
Than the characters in it
But it's speaking
About you, about me, about us.
You're not alone, I'm not alone
We've been in this together all along.

Please consider leaving a review on Amazon and Goodreads. A few words will help tremendously ♥

About The Author

*Amna Dhanani was 11 years old when she
wrote something for the first time without
being asked to. It was an article about
mothers, inspired by her mother.
Subsequently, as she was praised for that
article, she realized she could write and that's
how her journey as a writer began,
a journey in which she wishes to touch your
soul with her words.*

*She has only studied till 8th grade in school.
Since then, she has learned almost everything
on her own, often with no help from others.
Her keen observation of the world around her
taught her a lot.*

*Amna Dhanani, 25, is a diligent and
passionate writer from a small town in Sindh,
Pakistan. She writes about her perception of
the world, its love and beauty but also about
its pain and suffering which causes
heartbreak and teaches us the wisdom life
demands for survival.*

About The Book

My Existence Craves Yours is about how one heart seeks out the other in love, as if you're drought and they're rain. It's a story that contains true love, trauma of a broken heart, mental illness, imprisonment of one's soul and lessons of life.

Amna Dhanani says,
"I went through my work trying to come up with a theme, I wrecked my brain for weeks until I saw a pattern for a story. I've arranged the poems in a way that each poem has a place in the flow, even though the order that I've made is fictional but I've not only felt but lived every word that is in here, some by me and some by others as I couldn't stop myself from writing what my eyes saw, what my ears heard and what my heart felt through the pain of those around me. It often made my own existence suffer from their grief.

After the story, I've shared bits and pieces about my suffering and survival, ending on *The Words* chapter."